I0104750

Contents

„Anti-Zionism Is Anti-Semitism" 3

It Was Never About Hostages. It Was Never About Hamas.   4

Israel Will Even Persecute Palestinians For Simply Talking To Journalists
5

Waking Up From The Nightmare Of Western Civilization   7

Trump Backs Down On Yemen While India Bombs Pakistan   8

Israel Really Is As Evil As It Looks   10

India-Pakistan Ceasefire, And Other Notes From The Edge Of The Narrative Matrix   12

It Is Freakish And Insane How Our Society Averts Its Gaze From Gaza 14

Multiple Western Press Outlets Have Suddenly Pivoted Hard Against Israel
16

How To Make Your Mind Harder For The Propagandists To Manipulate   18

Israel Admits It Bombed A Hospital To Kill A Journalist For Doing Journalism   20

Never, Ever Let Anyone Forget What They Did To Gaza   22

Imagine If Gaza Was Jewish And The People Bombing It Were Muslims
23

THIS month's issue features a painting based on a photo from Palestinian journalist Moaz Abutaha, and it's titled "Never Forget What They Did To Gaza." Because we must never, ever let anyone forget.

I will spend the rest of my life reminding the world what these bastards did to Gaza. No matter what happens and regardless of how this thing plays out, I will never, ever let anyone forget how the empire inflicted all these months of horror upon all those innocent people.

The US-centralized western empire has demonstrated that it must cease to exist. The apartheid state of Israel has demonstrated that it must be dismantled. There is no coming back from this. Their crimes are unforgivable, and will never be forgotten.

All works are written by Caitlin Johnstone and Tim Foley. The Caitlin Johnstone project is 100 percent reader-funded. Cover is an original oil portrait of Francesca Albanese by Caitlin Johnstone.

Visit caitlinjohnst.one for the original articles and their supporting links.

Prostate Cancer Has A Right To Exist. Biden's Tumor Has A Right To Defend Itself.   24

You Are Already Fully Qualified To Oppose The Genocide In Gaza   26

Israeli Officials Explain Balancing Act Between Overt Genocide And Maintaining Western Support   28

The World Cannot Know True Peace Until We Have Reckoned With What We Did To Gaza   30

Israel Is A Uniquely Evil Society   31

The Western Media Brought Gaza To This Point   33

Thoughts On The Israeli Embassy Staff Killings   34

Today's Hitler Says „Free Palestine" Is Today's „Heil Hitler"   36

It's A Complete Lie To Say Gaza Can Have Peace If Hamas Surrenders 37

If You Don't Oppose The Gaza Holocaust, You've Been Wasting Your Life On This Planet   39

This Dystopia Would Never Be Accepted Without Extensive Indoctrination 40

Sorry If This Is Antisemitic But I Think It's Wrong To Burn Children Alive 41

If This Is What Israel Does, Then Israel Shouldn't Exist   43

Gaza's Hospitals ARE The Target 45

"Anti–Zionism Is Anti–Semitism"

Anti-Zionism is anti-semitism, you say? Sure, that makes sense. How someone prays and what religious beliefs they hold is exactly the same as supporting apartheid and genocide. You can't even tell them apart; the last time I tried to pray the rosary I got confused and bombed a children's hospital.

It's true: there is absolutely no difference whatsoever between opposing a political ideology and opposing the existence of a small religious minority. That's why it is universally considered racist to criticize an opposing political party. That's why anyone who tries to engage in a political debate is immediately arrested for committing a hate crime.

Anti-Zionism is anti-semitism. If you don't support the idea of dropping a western settler-colonialist state on top of a pre-existing civilization and then defending its status quo of apartheid, theft and abuse by any amount of violence necessary, then obviously you support the idea of exterminating millions of Jews in gas chambers.

If you don't want anyone to commit genocide against Palestinians, then that means you want to commit genocide against Jews. There is no third possibility.

Don't think we should be sending billions of dollars worth of military explosives to be dropped on hospitals, residential buildings and civilian infrastructure in Gaza? That means you harbor extremely negative emotions toward a small Abrahamic faith.

Think it's bad to deliberately starve millions of people who are trapped in a giant death camp? Then that means you want to start loading Jews onto trains.

Think it's wrong to wage a systematic extermination campaign against an entire people because they are a different ethnicity? Then you, sir, are no different from the Nazis.

Anti-Zionism is anti-semitism. Cats are ducks. The Declaration of Independence is spaghetti sauce. The Bronze Age is a foot fetish. There are no differences between any two things. All things are exactly the same as all other things.

The human mind is incapable of making any distinctions of any kind. Turning left is the same as turning right. Drinking water is the same as drinking bleach. Going to the supermarket is the same as killing your dad. This is how we all live our lives. Everyone knows this.

Everything I just said makes perfect sense. Anyone who disagrees is Hitler.

It Was Never About Hostages. It Was Never About Hamas.

Benjamin Netanyahu said on Thursday that freeing the Israeli hostages in Gaza was not his top priority, suggesting instead that defeating Hamas should take precedence over a hostage deal.

"We have many objectives, many goals in this war," Netanyahu said. "We want to bring back all of our hostages. That is a very important goal. In war, there is a supreme objective. And that supreme objective is victory over our enemies. And that is what we will achieve."

Nothing the prime minister said here is true or valid — unless by "enemies" he means "all Palestinians in the Gaza Strip".

Netanyahu has been fairly transparent about the fact that Israel's ultimate goal in Gaza is neither freeing the hostages nor defeating Hamas, but seizing Palestinian territory and removing its Palestinian inhabitants. He has openly said that Israel will occupy Gaza via military force, completely ruling out the possibility of any form of Palestinian government for the enclave. He has openly said he wants to enact President Donald Trump's ethnic cleansing plan for Gaza, which explicitly entails removing "all" Palestinians and never allowing them to return.

So they've made this perfectly clear. This isn't about Hamas, except insofar as an armed resistance group will make it difficult to forcibly remove all Palestinians from Gaza. And it certainly isn't about hostages.

And yet, bizarrely, this is how the western political-media class continues to frame this onslaught. They call it Israel's "war with Hamas", when it's nothing other than an undisguised ethnic cleansing operation. They prattle on about October 7, hostages, and terrorism, even though it has already been made abundantly clear that this has nothing to do with any of those things. They act as though the admission was simply never made.

There is absolutely no excuse for continuing to babble about hostages and Hamas after the US and Israel said the goal is the complete ethnic cleansing of Gaza. They told you what this is really about. They said it. With their face holes. They said it right to you. End of debate.

Israel has been seeking ways to purge Gaza of Palestinians for generations. That's all this has ever been about. Not October 7. Not hostages. Not Hamas. Not terrorism. Everything about Israel's operations in Gaza have indicated that their real goal is to remove Palestinians from a Palestinian territory and not to free hostages or defeat Hamas. And then when Trump took office, they started openly admitting it.

How is this not the whole entire conversation every time Gaza comes up? How is this not the beginning, middle and end of every single discussion?

This is like a cop looking right into someone's phone camera while strangling a black man to death and saying "I am killing this man because I am racist and I want to kill black people," and then afterward everyone's still saying "resisting arrest" and "we don't know what happened before the video started recording". He said what he was doing and what his motives were with his own mouth.

You don't get to babble about Hamas, October 7 or hostages in defense of Israel's actions in Gaza anymore. That is not a thing. If you want to defend Israel's actions in Gaza, the sole topic of conversation is whether or not it's okay to forcibly purge an entire population from their historic homeland by systematically bombing, shooting and starving them while destroying their civilian infrastructure, solely because of their ethnicity.

That is what the discussion is about. Not anything else. That and that only.

Feature image via Wikimedia Commons.

Israel Will Even Persecute Palestinians For Simply Talking To Journalists
•Notes From The Edge Of The Narrative Matrix•

Israeli soldiers have been harassing a Palestinian activist who appeared in Louis Theroux's recent documentary The Settlers to talk about Israel's apartheid abuses in the occupied West Bank. Issa Amro shared footage of IDF troops raiding his home over the weekend, days after Theroux's film debuted on the BBC.

Israelis not only murder journalists, attack journalistic institutions and block journalists from entering the Gaza Strip, they also persecute Palestinian civilians who speak with journalists.

If you haven't yet watched The Settlers, I highly recommend doing so. It's so damning that I've seen people expressing astonishment that it made it past the BBC's censors, but really, what's to censor? It's an hour of Israelis telling a video camera what Israelis think in their own words.

One of the best ways to tell the truth about the real Israel is to just point a camera at these freaks and let them tell it themselves. Theroux's interviewing style lends itself particularly well to this type of exposure.

•

A ship trying to bring humanitarian aid to Gaza was drone bombed by Israel near Malta on Friday. Activist Greta Thunberg was preparing to board the ship to travel with it to its destination.

Which is just wild to think about. Things are so fucked up on this timeline that there is a non-zero probability that Israel ends up assassinating Greta Thunberg.

Imagine the western reaction if Iran had bombed a humanitarian aid ship trying to feed starving civilians.

Imagine the reaction if Chinese forces were caught massacring medical workers in ambulances.

Imagine the reaction if Russia bombed an international humanitarian aid convoy in clearly marked vehicles.

It would be all we'd hear about for weeks.

•

My social media feeds are filling up with footage of skeletal starving children in Gaza. If we had sane and responsible news media in the west, this would be the lead story in every outlet and publication. But we do not have sane and responsible news media. We have propaganda services disguised as news media.

People who continue to support Israel are only able to do so because they actively avoid watching the video footage the rest of us are watching.

•

If I built a home and then discovered that it could only remain standing if I constantly massacred children, I would simply change my living arrangements.

I would not claim my building "has a right to exist".

I would not spend years explaining why my child massacres are okay.

I would not spend decades accusing anyone who criticized my child massacres of unfair discrimination against me and my family.

I would simply change my building so that its existence no longer required me to routinely massacre children. If I could not find a way to restructure my building in this way, I would move.

I would not do this because I am a remarkably kind and special person. I would do it because I am not a psychopath.

Only a psychopath would want to continue living in that kind of building. Only a psychopath would want that kind of building to remain standing.

•

I said the preceding on Twitter yesterday and Israel apologists immediately came in yelling at me for saying evil things about Israel, but what's funny is that I never mentioned Israel once; I just talked about a building. They only knew I was actually talking about Israel because of all the stuff I said about constantly massacring civilians.

Gets 'em every time.

•

It's good that Trump's "MAGA" base opposes war with Iran so forcefully, but it's pretty revealing how absent they've been on Trump's butchery in Yemen and Gaza. They're not opposed to war or mass murder, they're just opposed to fighting people who are strong enough to fight back.

Waking Up From The Nightmare Of Western Civilization

We don't need horror movies. We're creating our own horrors in places like Gaza.

We don't need dystopian fiction. We're living in dystopia right here in our own society.

We don't need fantasy stories about scary monsters. The scary monsters run our government.

Westerners will create a waking nightmare, psychologically compartmentalize away from its existence, and then go watch a movie about a fictional waking nightmare to give themselves a thrill.

We'll sit on the edge of our seats watching made-up tales about psychopathic killers while psychopathic killers rule the world.

We'll turn our backs on horrific acts of human butchery and then go watch fictional acts of human butchery, getting ourselves through any discomfort we might experience by reminding ourselves that what we are watching isn't happening in real life.

Someone in my Substack comments just asked me if I'd considered the possibility that the world might be better off without humanity, because of all the horrible things that are happening while the vast majority of us do nothing to stop it.

There are certainly many ugly things about human behavior, and there are forces within us which absolutely do not deserve to exist. Our self-centeredness. Our competitiveness. Our hatred and prejudice. Our seemingly limitless tolerance for unfathomable abuses so long as they are being inflicted on people in other countries whose anguished faces we don't have to look at. The delusions and trauma-based conditioning patterns we've been passing on from generation to generation since the dawn of civilization. The world would be better off without these things.

But over the years I have also become acquainted with dynamics inside the human organism which could make this world into a paradise, if we can only get out from underneath our delusion-based conditioning enough to realize them. Within every human being sleeps the potential for selfless action and vast compassion. We all have within us the ability to heal. We all have within us the ability to shed egoic consciousness like a reptile sheds old scales.

Maybe it's silly, but I like to think of this potentiality as a kind of Chekhov's gun for our species, sitting there onstage waiting to go off as humanity's story unfolds. I know for a fact that humans have the potential to awaken from the trance of the ego in profoundly transformative ways, and I choose to believe that the playwright put that potential there for a reason.

Every species eventually hits a point where it must adapt to changing conditions which threaten its existence or go extinct. It just happens that in humanity's case, the changing conditions which threaten our existence are the creations of our own minds. Ecocide. Nuclear brinkmanship. Weaponized AI. Biological warfare. The further our egos carry us down the path of competition and domination, the more likely it is that we open up some existential peril down the road for ourselves that there is no coming back from.

We'll either make the necessary adaptations and find a way to collectively unlock our dormant potential for selfless functioning on this planet, or we will go the way of the dinosaur. I keep at this because I have seen far too many strange and miraculous things in my life to believe such an awakening is impossible.

And the good news is we have truth on our side. The human ego is an illusion; the self does not exist. Enlightenment is already here, closer to us than our own breath, just being overlooked amid the flailings of the deluded mind. The propaganda is deceitful, and the truth is getting more and more exposure. Humans are getting better and better at sharing ideas and information about what's really happening in our world.

We just need to open our eyes. We just need to let truth get a word in edgewise. That's all that needs to happen.

We need to stop fixating on all these made up stories in our heads and on our screens, and look deeply at what's really going on.

Trump Backs Down On Yemen While India Bombs Pakistan
•Notes From The Edge Of The Narrative Matrix•

As if there's not enough terrible shit going on in the world right now, India has just bombed Pakistan. Both India and Pakistan are nuclear-armed states.

Missile strikes from India reportedly struck nine locations in Pakistan and Pakistani Kashmir, which India claims were "known terror camps". The strikes follow a terror attack in Indian Kashmir which India has blamed on Pakistan, while Islamabad has denied any involvement.

Pakistan has called the strikes "an act of war" and vowed to retaliate, claiming Indian planes were shot down during the attack. As of this writing there is some online footage which seems to corroborate claims of downed planes.

Nuclear states getting into tit-for-tat bombing exchanges with each other is a threat to everybody. This is a conflict that's been going on a long time, but as nuclear standoffs go this one is still relatively young (Pakistan tested its first nukes in 1998), so there are still a lot of uncharted waters here, and a lot that could go wrong if things continue to escalate. Hopefully this cools down as soon as possible.

In some positive news, the Trump administration has announced that it will stop bombing Yemen, finally accepting the longstanding offer from Ansar Allah to cease attacking US ships if the US ends its bombing campaign.

This is being framed as a victory for the US by Trump and his supporters, with Trump claiming the Houthis "capitulated", but if anything it's actually a win for Yemen. Yemeni forces have made it clear that they will continue attacking Israel until it halts its genocidal atrocities in Gaza, which was the only reason the US started bombing Yemen in the first place, and those attacks were the only reason Yemen was attacking American ships. After losing two fighter jets and more than twenty MQ-9 Reaper drones to Houthi attacks, the US is now retreating with its tail between its legs without having gained anything.

•

•

The Israeli government has approved a plan for the full military occupation of Gaza, which will reportedly include flattening every building that remains standing and concentrating the entire population into a single area while pressuring them to leave.

This has of course been the plan all along, but there's been a conspiracy of silence by the entire western political/media class against coming right out and saying so. Every journalist, pundit, politician and hasbarist throughout the western world has insisted on babbling about Hamas and hostages to explain Israel's actions in the Gaza Strip, when it's been clear from day one that this is really about ethnically cleansing and colonizing a Palestinian territory.

Now you've got Israeli Finance Minister Bezalel Smotrich coming right out and saying that the entire Gaza Strip will be "totally destroyed" and the Palestinian population "concentrated" into a small area at the southern tip of the enclave, while Israeli TV producer Elad Barashi openly calls for there to be a "Holocaust in Gaza" complete with "gas showers".

Zionists will say things like this in public while also telling you it's a hate crime to compare Israel to Nazi Germany.

•

More and more Palestinians are starving to death as Israel's total siege on the Gaza Strip continues. They're really going to deliberately starve Gaza with siege warfare and then say they need to empty out Gaza to rescue all those poor Palestinians from starvation.

•

Scientists are reporting a stunning 63 percent decline in populations of flying insects in the United Kingdom since 2021. Everyone focuses on climate change, but there are many, many other indications that our biosphere is in rapid decline which have little or nothing to do with global warming.

The first indication that space colonization is fiction is that they're talking about turning the desert planet Mars into a thriving biosphere while we're turning our own thriving biosphere into a desert planet.

•

Israel Really Is As Evil As It Looks

Israeli snipers routinely, deliberately shoot children in the head throughout the Gaza Strip.

Israel created an AI system for the IDF to target suspected Hamas fighters when they go home to their families and mockingly called it "Where's Daddy?", because they are killing the fighters' children.

Israel has targeted healthcare facilities and ambulances in Gaza hundreds upon hundreds of times. They've been documented entering the hospitals they attack and systematically destroying individual pieces of medical equipment in order to make them unusable.

IDF soldiers constantly post photos and videos to their social media accounts showing themselves mockingly dressing in the clothes of dead and displaced Palestinian women and playing with the toys of dead and displaced Palestinian children.

The IDF has admitted to running a popular Telegram channel called "72 Virgins" which posted extremely gory and sadistic snuff films of people in Gaza being butchered by Israeli forces.

After destroying buildings full of civilians, the IDF has been known to send in sniper drones to pick off the survivors, including children.

Israel has murdered a historically unprecedented number of journalists in its Gaza onslaught, and has been knowingly attacking humanitarian aid workers.

Israeli soldiers rape and torture Palestinian prisoners to death, including doctors. On the rare occasions that anyone is ever arrested for these abuses, Israelis have riots — not to oppose the abuses, but to oppose the arrests of the perpetrators.

And now Israel is openly declaring its agenda to ethnically cleanse the entire Gaza Strip of Palestinians, with Finance Minister Bezalel Smotrich saying the plan is for Gaza's population to be "concentrated" at the southern end of the enclave and pressured to leave while the rest of Gaza is "totally destroyed".

"The population of Gaza will be concentrated from the Morag Corridor southwards. The rest of the Strip will be empty," Smotrich said, adding, "They will be totally despairing, understanding that there is no hope and nothing to look for in Gaza, and will be looking for relocation to begin a new life in other places."

A poll released earlier this year found that only three percent of Jewish Israelis oppose the planned ethnic cleansing of Gaza on moral grounds. That's right: three percent. Three out of every one hundred people.

I got into a back and forth with a liberal Israel supporter the other day whose entire argument basically boiled down to "Oh so you're claiming Israel is just doing terrible things to civilians on purpose, just because they're evil??"

And, I mean, yes. That's a bit of an oversimplification, but yes. Israel is evil. It's a deeply evil country full of deeply evil people. Again: three percent.

My interlocutor was attempting to dismiss the idea of Israelis being horrible people as a legitimate explanation for their actions in Gaza, meaning Israel's actions could only be explained as rational responses to unfortunate provocations by the Palestinians (who he of course had no trouble believing were bloodthirsty savages). But the evidence says Israel really is as evil as it looks.

As we have discussed previously, this isn't because there's anything inherently evil in Judaism or Jewishness which would cause a state led by Jews to behave in this way. Rather, it's because modern Israel has from its very inception been premised on the idea of a tiered society where one ethnic group dominates the others, making injustice and inequality an inherent part of the system. Israelis are indoctrinated from birth into accepting this unjust apartheid framework as normal, which necessarily entails indoctrinating them into accepting the dehumanization and abuse of the disempowered group.

If you have a society whose populace are systematically indoctrinated into accepting apartheid and abuse as normal and good, you are inevitably going to wind up with a society full of sociopaths. That's who's going to be casting the votes, serving in the military, working in the media, and working in the government. It's not caused by their ethnicity or their religion — it's caused by the perverse nature of the apartheid state in which they live.

Many westerners tend to give Israel the benefit of the doubt because they assume from the beginning that this can't be as simple as it looks and the abuse cannot be as one-sided as it appears to be. They assume this because western news media and politicians are constantly churning out narratives to make Israel look as innocent as possible and Palestinians look as guilty as possible, but in reality this really is exactly what it looks like: Israelis murdering and starving a civilian population in order to steal their land.

It really is that simple. Israel really is that bad. And so is anyone who supports it.

India–Pakistan Ceasefire, And Other Notes From The Edge Of The Narrative Matrix

After a few frightening missile and drone strike exchanges and some of the most large-scale aerial combat that our world has seen in recent history, India and Pakistan have reportedly agreed to a full and immediate ceasefire.

So that's a relief. I was about to publish a piece about this conflict and the risk of nuclear war when the ceasefire was announced, and I've never in my life been so happy to have to throw out hours of my work. Things are still tense and the grievances of Kashmiris under Indian occupation remain unaddressed, but at least the nuclear brinkmanship is de-escalating for today.

•

In more good news, a judge has ordered the release of Rumeysa Ozturk, the Tufts University student who the Trump administration had detained for deportation solely for publishing an op-ed critical of Israel. When dismissing the case the judge actually said "there has been no evidence that has been introduced by the government other than the op-ed — I mean, that literally is the case."

Imagine trying to put together a compelling legal argument only to have a judge squint at it, read out your reasoning, and then just say "I mean, that literally is the case" before throwing it out.

It's good that Trump's efforts to criminalize criticism of Israel keep faceplanting in the courts, but in a sense the damage has already been done. Non-citizens in the US are going to be far more reluctant to speak out against Israel's US-backed crimes for fear of persecution.

Judges have ordered the release of Ozturk and Mohsen Mahdawi in their respective cases, ruling their persecution for political speech unlawful. Other judges have given smaller wins to pro-Palestine activists like Mahmoud Khalil and Badar Khan Suri, but they remain in detention. All of them have spent weeks locked up like criminals for their speech and activism opposing an active genocide.

That alone would be enough to dissuade many non-citizens from speaking out about the Gaza holocaust while in the United States. A chilling effect has already taken place, because many people are unwilling to risk weeks or months in a cage while the world's most murderous and tyrannical government works to deport them to another country — even if they might wind up winning in the courts eventually.

This chilling effect is a theft of the rights of US citizens as well as non-citizens, because it robs citizens of their right to hear what these activists have to say. Their government stepped in and hid speech that is critical of US foreign policy from their ears, determining that it would be best if Americans did not consume such wrongthink. If this isn't tyranny, then nothing is.

Free speech is being stomped out throughout the western world to protect Israel and its western backers from criticism. There is no greater threat to the right to free expression in our society today. It must be opposed, and opposed ferociously.

•

Haaretz reports that the Israeli military has placed returning the hostages at the very bottom of its list of priorities in Gaza, with items like "concentration and movement of the public" and "operational control of the territory" ranking as more important goals.

The correct response to anyone who babbles about hostages when you criticize Israel's actions in Gaza is "Shut the fuck up you lying genocidal sack of shit." It was never about the hostages. Everyone knows it was never about the hostages. It was always about ethnic cleansing.

•

Americans and Israelis have been butchering people throughout west Asia with increasing brazenness and aggression, and yet people will still expect to be taken seriously when they tell you that you should be afraid of Muslims.

•

We've been seeing some unexpected voices suddenly coming out and denouncing Israel's genocide in Gaza and admitting that they were wrong for supporting it, including the Financial Times editorial board, Conservative MP Mark Pritchard, and Israeli academic Shaiel Ben-Ephraim.

I don't want to get anyone's hopes up, but it would be good if this was a sign of something shifting.

•

It Is Freakish And Insane How Our Society Averts Its Gaze From Gaza

It can make you feel like you're going mad. How phony and superficial it all is. How we're a year and a half into history's first live-streamed genocide and our whole society is acting like everything's peachy.

We're murdering kids. We're starving them. We're dropping high tech military explosives on them. Blowing their limbs off. Ripping their guts out. Shooting them in the head. This isn't just being done by "Israel". It's being done by the entire western empire which backs these atrocities.

And yet if you turn on a TV you'll see famous people laughing and joking about nonsense, expressing political opinions of no more depth and significance than whether or not there should have been a female Ghostbusters movie. Go read the news and it's dominated by empty fluff about celebrities and politicians and the latest brain fart to come out of Donald Trump's mouth. Go to a party and everyone's nattering about vapid gibberish, yelling "No politics!" if you try to say anything about the holocaust-shaped elephant in the room.

Newer readers might not know this, but I used to have a lot more fun on my platform. Lots of humor. Psychedelic poetry. Spirituality and philosophy. But ever since the Gaza holocaust began, that kind of writing has often felt like it would be irreverent and frivolous. Almost sacrilegious. I would feel like I'm joining in with the madness of mainstream culture by turning my back on all those emaciated bodies and mutilated children.

So for the last year and a half I've mostly just been doing what I feel everyone on earth ought to be doing: pointing to the genocide and saying it needs to stop.

I used to be a lot more poetical and creative in my ways of pointing to the criminality of the empire, because its depravity was often difficult for people to really grasp, so I was always seeking out new ways to help people see its monstrosity with fresh eyes. Now that they're just butchering children right in front of us, that's not really what's called for anymore. What's called for is to keep drawing everyone's attention to the terrible thing that's staring us all right in the face.

This task shouldn't be falling to university activists and obscure antiwar bloggers. Every news outlet in the world should be making this their entire focus.

If we had a sane and ethical news media, this is what they would be doing. All the leading stories every single day would be about the latest evil thing Israel and its western backers have done in Gaza, clearly stating in every headline our own government's role in making this possible. Every press conference would be completely dominated with questions asking every western official why we are participating in an active genocide and demanding answers about when it is going to stop.

Instead we get "Palestinians perish in explosion" passive-language headlines, usually coupled with "… says Hamas-run health ministry" in order to let readers disbelieve the entire story. And that's on those rare occasions that Israel's atrocities get reported on at all; normally Gaza is seen as a third or fourth-tier issue of far less importance than some infinitely less egregious grievance in our own country. Palestinian lives are given vastly less weight than western lives, with our own feelings and comforts emphasized far more heavily than the issue of the Palestinian people living or dying.

And it can just make you feel like you're going crazy. It's like if we were all going around physically drenched in human blood, with blood flooding our living rooms and severed limbs strewn about our bedrooms and kitchens — but nobody was talking about it. You try to say "What's up with all this blood and gore?" and they shush you and tell you it's impolite to talk about politics. A dark red deluge pours out of your minivan door when you open it to pick up your kid from soccer practice, and everyone looks away.

This is happening. We know it's happening. It's happening right in front of us and we're acting like it's not. It's so maddening and frustrating, and it can make you feel so powerless.

But we keep pointing at Gaza, because what the hell else are we going to do? The alternative is to join the lunatics acting like it isn't happening.

At the very least, it's a way of preserving our sanity. Preserving our humanity. Even if they do succeed in purging Gaza of all Palestinian life, at the very least we will have prevented the bastards from warping and twisting us into psychopathic freaks like them. Even if we can't stop them from destroying Gaza, we can at least stop them from destroying our hearts.

Multiple Western Press Outlets Have Suddenly Pivoted Hard Against Israel

After a year and a half of genocidal atrocities, the editorial boards of numerous British press outlets have suddenly come out hard against Israel's genocidal onslaught in Gaza.

The first drop of rain came last week from The Financial Times in a piece by the editorial board titled "The west's shameful silence on Gaza," which denounces the US and Europe for having "issued barely a word of condemnation" of their ally's criminality, saying they "should be ashamed of their silence, and stop enabling Netanyahu to act with impunity."

Then came The Economist with a piece titled "The war in Gaza must end," which argues that Trump should pressure the Netanyahu regime for a ceasefire, saying that "The only people who benefit from continuing the war are Mr Netanyahu, who keeps his coalition intact, and his far-right allies, who dream of emptying Gaza and rebuilding Jewish settlements there."

On Saturday came an editorial from The Independent titled "End the deafening silence on Gaza — it is time to speak up," arguing that British PM Keir Starmer "should be ashamed that he said nothing, especially since Mr Netanyahu has now announced new plans to expand the already devastating bombardment of Gaza," and saying that "It is time for the world to wake up to what is happening and to demand an end to the suffering of the Palestinians trapped in the enclave."

On Sunday The Guardian editorial board joined in with a write-up titled "The Guardian view on Israel and Gaza: Trump can stop this horror. The alternative is unthinkable," saying "The US president has the leverage to force through a ceasefire. If he does not, he will implicitly signal approval of what looks like a plan of total destruction."

"What is this, if not genocidal?" The Guardian asks. "When will the US and its allies act to stop the horror, if not now?"

To be clear, these are editorials, not op-eds. This means that they are not the expression of one person's opinion but the stated position of each outlet as a whole. We've been seeing the occasional op-ed which is critical of Israel's actions throughout the Gaza holocaust in the mainstream western press, but to see the actual outlets come out aggressively denouncing Israel and its western backers all at once is a very new development.

Some longtime Israel supporters have unexpectedly begun changing their tune as individuals as well.

Conservative MP Mark Pritchard said at the House of Commons last week that he had supported Israel "at all costs" for decades, but said "I got it wrong" and publicly withdrew that support over Israel's actions in Gaza.

"For many years — I've been in this House twenty years — I have supported Israel pretty much at all costs, quite frankly," Pritchard said. "But today, I want to say that I got it wrong and I condemn Israel for what it is doing to the Palestinian people in Gaza and indeed in the West Bank, and I'd like to withdraw my support right now for the actions of Israel, what they are doing right now in Gaza."

"I'm really concerned that this is a moment in history when people look back, where we've got it wrong as a country," Pritchard added.

Pro-Israel pundit Shaiel Ben-Ephraim, who had been aggressively denouncing campus protesters and accusing Israel's critics of "blood libel" throughout the Gaza holocaust, has now come out and publicly admitted that Israel is committing a genocide which must be opposed.

"It took me a long time to get to this point, but it's time to face it. Israel is committing genocide in Gaza," Ephraim tweeted recently. 'Between the indiscriminate bombing of hospitals, starvation of the population, plans for ethnic cleansing, slaughter of aid workers and cover ups, there is no escaping it. Israel is trying to eradicate the Palestinian people. We can't stop it unless we admit it."

It is odd that it has taken all these people a year and a half to get to this point. I myself have a much lower tolerance for genocide and the mass murder of children. If you've been riding the genocide train for nineteen months, it looks a bit weird to suddenly start screaming about how terrible it is and demanding to hit the brakes all of a sudden.

These people have not suddenly evolved a conscience, they're just smelling what's in the wind. Once the consensus shifts past a certain point there's naturally going to be a mad rush to avoid being among the last to

stand against it, because you know you'll be wearing that mark for the rest of your life in public after history has had a clear look at what you did.

This is after all coming at a time when the Trump administration is beginning to rub Netanyahu's fur the wrong way, recently prompting the Israeli prime minister to say "I think we'll have to detox from US security assistance" when Washington went over Tel Aviv's head and negotiated directly with Hamas to secure the release of an American hostage. The US is reportedly leaving Israel out of more and more of its negotiations on international affairs in places like Yemen and Iran. Something is changing.

So if you're still supporting Israel after all this time, my advice to you is to make a change while you still can. There's still time to be the first among scoundrels in the mad rat race to avoid being the last to start acting like you always opposed the Gaza holocaust.

How To Make Your Mind Harder For The Propagandists To Manipulate

The worst mistake you can make when reading the news is to assume there's a good reason why the mass media report on something in the way that they do. That there's a good reason why Israel-Palestine gets framed as a complex and morally ambiguous issue with no clear path forward, even though it all looks pretty self-evident to you. That there must be a valid and legitimate reason why one story gets more coverage than a seemingly far more important story, like how the release of one Israeli-American hostage is currently getting far more news media coverage than the deliberate starvation of an entire enclave full of civilians.

In reality there is no valid and legitimate reason why such things are covered the way they are. The coverage happens in the way that it happens because it serves the information interests of Israel and the western empire, and for no other reason.

So much western ignorance is facilitated by the manipulative way the imperial media report on what's going on in the world. People assume that because they're not hearing about a given issue all the time or in a particularly urgent tone of reporting, it must not be an especially important matter that needs their attention. They assume that if one side of a conflict isn't framed as being clearly in the wrong, then it must not be.

Westerners assume that if the world were experiencing another Holocaust, another Transatlantic Slave Trade, another Cuban Missile Crisis, they would hear about it in the news at an appropriate level of urgency. But that simply isn't how it works. The only reason the western public is ever told about anything bad that happens at a high level of frequency and urgency is when it is convenient for the western empire, like when Russia invaded Ukraine. When that happened it was the main story in every western outlet for ages, and Russia was clearly framed as the evil aggressor, with all the NATO aggressions which provoked the invasion going completely unmentioned.

When people hear the word "propaganda" they tend to think it means the same thing as "lies", but that's not accurate. The domestic propaganda that westerners are fed by the powerful does not typically consist of whole-cloth fabrications, but rather of distortions, half-truths, manipulated emphasis, and lies by omission.

Most of the worst things the US and its allies are doing in the world are reported accurately by the western press at certain times and in certain publications, but they simply are not given any emphasis and amplification after those brief mentions. If you look at the hyperlinks I cite in my articles to describe the criminality of the empire it's usually either straight out of the mainstream press or some other independent author who's citing mainstream news reporting. The difference is that I regularly spotlight those admissions, while the imperial media will mention them once halfway down an article somewhere and then let the daily news churn carry it away down the memory hole.

Western propaganda doesn't consist so much of manipulating what gets reported but how it gets reported. How often something gets mentioned. How often the perpetrator of an abuse is explicitly named. The type of language used to describe a given offense. These adjustments might sound insignificant when they are described, but when put into practice across the board they are extremely effective at shaping public perception of world affairs.

The only way to get around this is to maintain an acute awareness of what's being reported while ignoring distorting factors like frequency, emphasis and tone. You have to just focus on the raw data of what's being reported about what the empire is up to from day to day without allowing your perception to be colored by the way in which that data is reported. If you come across a key piece of information about the empire's criminality you've got to hold onto it and remember its significance for yourself, because the imperial press sure aren't going to remind you. They're going to be acting like it never happened by next week.

It's bizarre once you start noticing how much of a disconnect there is between reality and the mass media's reporting on world events. They'll occasionally mention actual important things, but there's no accurate sense of proportionality to any of it. It's like if you were at a restaurant with a friend and a waiter's uniform caught fire, and your friend just casually mentioned "Oh that guy's on fire" before going back to talking about the meal for the rest of the conversation while the guy burned to death at the other end of the room. It is utterly surreal.

So one of the most important things you need to do to maintain a truth-based worldview is to take complete control over your own understanding of the importance of the pieces of information which come across your field of vision. You can't rely on others to tell you how important they are, because all the most amplified and influential voices in our society are working to manipulate your understanding of their importance, and most ordinary people you'll interact with are being manipulated by those voices to some extent. Public political discourse is overwhelmingly dominated by these distortions.

You've got to interpret the urgency and importance of information for yourself. By standing on your own two feet and looking at the raw data with fresh eyes before it gets jumbled around by the imperial spin machine, you make your mind much harder to bend to the will of the empire.

Israel Admits It Bombed A Hospital To Kill A Journalist For Doing Journalism
•Notes From The Edge Of The Narrative Matrix•

The IDF has admitted to bombing a hospital in order to assassinate a prominent Palestinian journalist in Gaza, explicitly stating that they assassinated him for engaging in journalistic activities.

The official Israel Defense Forces account made the following post on Twitter (emphasis added):

"Don't let Aslih's press vest fool you:

Hassan Abdel Fattah Mohammed Aslih, a terrorist from the Hamas Khan Yunis brigade, was eliminated along with other terrorists in the 'Nasser' hospital in Khan Yunis.

Aslih participated in the brutal October 7 massacre under the guise of a journalist and owner of a news network. During the massacre, he documented acts of murder, looting, and arson, posting the footage online.

Journalist? More like terrorist."

Documenting newsworthy acts and posting the footage online is also known as journalism. It's the thing that journalism is.

Aslih was killed in the hospital's burn unit where he was recovering from a previous Israeli assassination attempt in which they bombed a tent near that same hospital.

That's right kids, Israel will literally assassinate a journalist by bombing a hospital, openly admit that they bombed the hospital to assassinate the journalist for engaging in journalistic activities — and then call you an antisemite if you say Israel bombs hospitals and assassinates journalists.

•

The following things are Hamas: journalists, journalism, the new pope, the last pope, the UN, Amnesty International, Human Rights Watch, human rights, critical thinking, hospitals, schools, campus protesters, Greta Thunberg, doctors, women, children, Ireland, and Ms Rachel.

•

Benjamin Netanyahu is now saying that the forced ethnic cleansing of Palestinians from Gaza was "inevitable," reportedly telling the Knesset's Foreign Affairs and Defense Committee on Sunday that "We are destroying more and more homes, and Gazans have nowhere to return to. The only inevitable outcome will be the wish of Gazans to emigrate outside of the Gaza Strip."

So there you have it. Shut the fuck up about hostages. Shut the fuck up about Hamas. Shut the fuck up about October 7. This is about removing Palestinians from a Palestinian territory to replace them with Jewish settlers. That's all this has ever been about. Anyone who pretends otherwise is evil.

•

"You support terrorism," said the person who supports daily massacres of civilians to advance political aims.

•

always get Israel apologists telling me "Stop calling it a genocide! It's not a genocide!"

And I'm always just like okay well then they're doing some sort of thing where the people in power work to eliminate a population because of their ethnicity using mass-scale violence and deliberate starvation. I guess there's no word for it.

•

Everyone's yelling about Trump accepting a jet from Qatar as a bribe, which would make sense if they hadn't been completely ignoring how Trump has openly admitted to being bought and controlled by the world's richest Israeli Miriam Adelson, and how pervasively influential the Israel lobby is throughout all of US politics.

It's so gross that western society tolerates the existence of an Israel lobby. Like "Oh so you're here to convince my government to stomp out my free speech rights and use my tax dollars for wars and genocide to advance the interests of an apartheid state? Yeah cool, I guess that's fine."

The existence of the Israel lobby should be treated the same as a Nazi lobby or a pedophilia lobby. Taking donations from pro-Israel groups should be as stigmatized as taking donations from the KKK or NAMBLA.

It's not okay that each western nation has its own high-powered lobby group whose whole entire job is to insert itself into key points of influence and persuade our governments to destroy our civil rights and commit genocide. Nobody should tolerate the existence of these groups.

•

IThe last year and a half in Gaza is a strong enough reason to dismantle the entire US-led western empire. The Gaza holocaust could end tomorrow and it would still be reason enough. All the empire's other worldwide abuses could have never happened and it'd still be reason enough.

In Gaza alone the empire has already established beyond any doubt that it should not exist, even if you ignore all its other crimes throughout the middle east, Latin America, Africa and Asia. If you would perpetrate history's first live-streamed genocide in full view of the entire world, then you are not the sort of power structure who should be leading humanity into the future. If you would inflict the kinds of abuses we've been watching on our screens for the last year and a half upon helpless human beings who have done nothing wrong, then you should not rule the world. Your rule must end.

The alternative is to let the fate of humanity be determined by genocidal monsters. This is simply not an option. The sooner the US-centralized empire ends, the better.

•

Never, Ever Let Anyone Forget What They Did To Gaza

I will never forget the Gaza holocaust. I will never let anyone else forget about the Gaza holocaust.

No matter what happens or how this thing turns out, I will never let anyone my voice touches forget that our rulers did the most evil things imaginable right in front of us and lied to us about it the entire time.

I will never stop doing everything I can with my own small platform to help ensure that the perpetrators of this mass atrocity are brought to justice.

I will never stop doing everything I can to help bring down the western empire and to help free Palestine from the Zionist entity.

I will never forget those shaking children. Those tiny shredded bodies. Those starved, skeletal forms. The explosions followed by screams. The atrocities followed by western media silence.

I will never forget, and I will never forgive. I will never forgive our leaders. I will never forgive the western press. I will never forgive Israel. I will never forgive the mainstream US political parties. I will always want for them exactly what they wanted for the Palestinians.

No matter what happens or what they do in the future, they will always be the people who did this to Gaza. They will always be the people who inflicted this nightmare upon our species. That will always be the most significant thing about them. It will always be the single most defining characteristic about who they are as human beings.

And the same is true of all the ordinary members of the public who continued to stand with Israel long after evidence of its criminality became undeniable. They are genocide supporters, first and foremost.

If you stood on the side of Israel during the Gaza holocaust, then that is the most important thing about you, and it always will be. It doesn't matter if you go to church on Sunday. It doesn't matter if you are nice to your children and your pets. It doesn't matter if you give money to charity, support local farmers, or drive an electric vehicle. The thing that matters most about you as a person is that you supported history's first live-streamed genocide, and it always will be the thing that matters most about you.

I will keep bringing this up. Year after year. Decade after decade. I will keep rubbing everyone's face in it. I will never tire of doing so. I will always do my part to remind the world who these people are, and what they did to Gaza.

•

Imagine If Gaza Was Jewish And The People Bombing It Were Muslims

Gaza just endured one of its worst days of bombing since the beginning of Israel's genocidal onslaught, with the IDF ramping up aggressions as it prepares for the full military capture of the enclave.

On Thursday the United Nations rejected the US-Israeli plan for delivering aid to the besieged Palestinian territory. The plan has been slammed as a transparent attempt to use food to lure Gaza's starving population southward into a concentrated area to prepare them for deportation, i.e. ethnic cleansing.

If Gaza was populated by Jews and the people massacring its inhabitants were Muslims, nobody would have any trouble calling this thing what it is. The words "genocide" and "Holocaust" would've been appearing in the news every single day for the last 19 months.

Except we all know it wouldn't have gone on for 19 months. In the eyes of the western empire, there are some people who may be murdered with mass military violence, and others who may not be. There are some types of children who can be photographed with their ribcages sticking out because of deliberately inflicted starvation without causing much of a stir, and there are other types of children for whom such photographs would shake the earth.

In the eyes of the western empire, Jews are considered fully human, while Muslims and Arabs are not. A massacre of Jews is a terrible, unforgivable atrocity which cries out to the heavens for limitless vengeance, while Israel's daily massacres of Palestinians merit nothing more than a footnote.

If Gaza was populated by Jews and the people conducting these daily massacres were Muslims, the western empire would have long ago intervened to stop this. Instead we get swamp monsters like Steve Witkoff recycling the bogus Biden administration line that "the Israeli government is a sovereign government; they can't tell us what to do and we can't tell them what to do," and Secretary of State Marco Rubio saying he's "concerned" about the humanitarian situation in Gaza but doesn't see any alternatives — just like his predecessor Antony Blinken constantly did.

It's so glaringly, painfully obvious what we're looking at. So completely blatant and undisguised. The only thing keeping people from seeing this genocide for what it is and calling a spade a spade is the fact that its victims happen to belong to a religion and an ethnicity that has been systematically dehumanized for decades in order to justify the acts of mass military violence that have been aggressively normalized in our collective psychology. Westerners have been indoctrinated by domestic propaganda into seeing Arabs and Muslims as less than human, in much the same way Israelis themselves have been.

It's so gross and uncomfortable to have to keep finding new ways to say "Imagine if this was happening to a population you actually care about," but it seems like that's the only way a lot of people are going to open their eyes and look at this thing. Until you begin to entertain the possibility that the people suffering in Gaza might actually be similar to you and the people you consider human, it's just going to be a big blind spot for you.

It should not be necessary to do this. It should be obvious to all of us that humans are humans regardless of their race or religion or any other way they might show up as a bit different from us. We should all have been taught this as young children.

But that's where we're at as a civilization right now. A genocide happening right in front of us, and people like me going "Imagine if they belonged to a religion that you HAVEN'T been trained to fear and despise!"

It's undignified, and it says ugly things about our society that this is still one of the most effective ways to get this message across. But we can only begin the journey toward a healthy world from where we are standing here and now.

•

Prostate Cancer Has A Right To Exist. Biden's Tumor Has A Right To Defend Itself.
•Notes From The Edge Of The Narrative Matrix•

Joe Biden reportedly has an aggressive form of prostate cancer which has spread to his bones.

On this day we must all stand in solidarity with Biden's cancerous growth. Prostate cancer has a right to exist. Biden's malignant metastatic tumor must be given everything it needs to defend itself from unprovoked attacks by radical oncologists.

•

None of the people wishing Biden well today have ever really stood for anything. Nobody who chides those who are celebrating his cancer diagnosis actually cares about human beings. They inhabit a different moral universe from the rest of us. One where politeness and decorum matter more than human lives. One where it's more important to preserve one's political image in the eyes of the establishment than it is to oppose an active genocide. One where a rude tweet about a blood-soaked monster provokes more outrage than daily footage of children ripped to shreds by western-supplied munitions.

Those who are applauding Biden's tumor today are obviously not saying that cancer is good. They are saying that Biden's victims matter more than the rules of imperial etiquette. They are saying the mountains of human corpses he created matter more than protecting the feelings of those who believe he's a swell guy. They are rejecting the empire's demand that they dehumanize and dismiss all those people who were killed, crippled, displaced, traumatized and bereaved by the abuses of this fugitive from The Hague in order to demonstrate docility and obedience to their masters.

When Biden finally dies there will be people falling all over themselves to sanctify his image and grieve him as a kind and beneficent leader, and there will be those lining up to piss on his grave. The latter group will be of far greater moral quality than the former, no matter what they try to tell you.

•

Israel has greatly escalated its murderous aggressions in Gaza in its efforts to fully capture the enclave and empty it of its inhabitants.

Opposing Israel's western-backed genocide in Gaza is the bare-minimum requirement for anyone to take you seriously on any other issue, in the same way nobody cares what a neo-Nazi thinks about healthcare or what someone who wants to abolish age of consent laws thinks about taxes.

•

Israel and its apologists permanently lost the argument as soon as they started telling you it's racist to oppose genocide. From that point on there was no reason to listen to them or engage them in any way.

•

They're trying to tell you that genocide is normal. THEY'RE TRYING TO TELL YOU THAT GENOCIDE IS NORMAL. Reject the mainstream western worldview. Everything you've been taught about the world is a lie.

•

Saying the US is "complicit" in the Gaza genocide is like saying Hitler was complicit in the Holocaust. This is the USA's genocide as much as it is Israel's.

If you saw one man holding someone down while another man slashes their throat, you wouldn't say you saw one murderer and one complicit bystander, you would say you saw someone being murdered by two men.

If you drove your friend to the house of someone you hate, helped him break in, tackled your victim together, handed your friend a knife, held your victim down while your friend slit their throat, and then drove the getaway car and helped your friend dispose of the evidence, nobody would describe you as merely "complicit" in that crime. If you were caught, you would both be charged with premeditated homicide, and everyone would view you as a murderer.

The US — and to a lesser extent its western allies — have been actively participating in this genocide since day one. They've been supplying the weapons. They've been providing military intelligence. They've been backing Israel in the UN. They've been bombing Yemen off and on to stop it from imposing a blockade in an effort to rescue Gaza. They've been providing political and diplomatic cover to ensure that the genocide can continue uninterrupted without any consequences.

Israeli military insiders have openly acknowledged that this genocide would have been impossible without Washington's backing. Both Biden and Trump have had the ability to end this nightmare at any time with a single phone call threatening to withhold aid if peace isn't made. Instead of making that call, they have continued knowingly and actively participating in the crime. Holding onto the struggling victim while the knife blade comes down.

The argument for the US-led world order is over. It's done. There is no coming back from this. That they would commit history's first live-streamed genocide in full view of the entire world means they cannot be left to lead the world any longer. The globe-spanning power structure that is loosely centralized around Washington must be brought down. Humanity has no future if these monsters are left in charge.

•

You Are Already Fully Qualified To Oppose The Genocide In Gaza

You don't need to understand every little detail about Israel and Palestine to oppose the genocide in Gaza. You can safely go with your gut on this one. You can and should research this issue, of course, but everything you learn will only make Israel look worse.

I say this because I see too many people get intimidated away from speaking out about Gaza by an erroneous but widespread notion that this is an issue best left to the experts. This notion is promulgated by Israel and its apologists throughout the western world, who try to frame this as a super duper complex issue which requires years of research to be able to comprehend with the requisite nuance and accuracy.

And it's complete bullshit. The Gaza genocide is exactly what it looks like at first glance. I say this as someone who has been researching this issue extensively.

You don't need to know everything about the history of modern Israel to know that it's wrong to intentionally starve a civilian population. You don't need to be able to defend your position to aggressive pro-Israel trolls online to know that it's wrong to assassinate journalists, bomb hospitals, and rain military explosives on areas full of children. You don't need any qualifications of any kind to see the horrific footage coming out of Gaza and denounce your government for facilitating those atrocities.

Israel and its supporters understand the power of narrative control better than maybe any other group out there. They even have a word, "hasbara", for the practice of defending Israel's public image and justifying its crimes to the western public. If you speak out about Gaza on any public forum you are likely to run into a hasbarist who tries to intimidate you into silence by knowing a little bit more than you about this issue and spouting a few talking points that you are not quite equipped to address just yet.

And I am telling you that you should definitely disregard these people and push past your initial impulse to be intimidated into silence. The reason "I ain't reading all that, free Palestine" has become a meme in pro-Palestine circles is because Israel apologists have been trying to use mountains of verbiage to counter the public response to raw video footage documenting clear abuses in Gaza. It takes a whole lot of words to try and spin footage of mutilated children as the fault of Hamas, or photos of IDF soldiers mockingly dressing in the clothes of dead and displaced Palestinian women as fine and normal. They confront people with walls of text filled with apologia and talking points to try and overwhelm their common sense and empathy as they look at raw evidence of Israel's depravity.

We saw a really glaring example of the way Israel's defenders try to intimidate people into silence with the recent debate on Joe Rogan between Israel apologist Douglas Murray and Israel critic Dave Smith. Murray spoke in a smug, condescending tone the entire time and tried to suggest that because Smith has never physically been to Gaza then he has no business publicly expressing an opinion about it.

This is self-evidently insane. Obviously you don't need to go to Gaza to know that the facts and footage you're seeing coming out of the enclave are awful. No matter how many times you go to Israel and the Palestinian territories, it will still be wrong to bomb hospitals and intentionally starve civilians and create the largest population of child amputees on this planet. But Israel's apologists are constantly using some version of this tactic to silence Israel's critics by implying that they don't have enough personal expertise on this issue to voice opposition to an active genocide.

Don't buy into it. Speak out against the Gaza holocaust, even if you aren't an expert and don't understand every little detail just yet. Definitely keep researching and learning, but please do not be intimidated into thinking you need to be some kind of doctorate-level scholar on this issue before you can publicly oppose history's first live-streamed genocide.

Israel's supporters want you to believe this so that you will shut up long enough for them to purge the Gaza Strip of all Palestinian life. Your hesitation buys them time to do this.

Disregard their intimidation tactics. Dismiss them, block them, move away from them, and continue opposing the genocide.

•

Israeli Officials Explain Balancing Act Between Overt Genocide And Maintaining Western Support

One of the talking points Israel apologists like to regurgitate is that Israel can't possibly be acting with genocidal intent in Gaza, because if they had wanted to exterminate the Palestinians they could have easily done so in a matter of days.

As luck would have it, leaders from the Israeli government have just helpfully come out and debunked that talking point with a few shockingly frank public admissions.

Explaining the decision to allow a minuscule amount of aid into Gaza after months of deliberate starvation, Prime Minister Benjamin Netanyahu said on Monday that Israel is now allowing "minimal humanitarian aid" on the insistence of western officials so that they will support Israel's murderous operation to conquer the enclave.

Jeremy Scahill reports the following for Drop Site News:

> "We're going to take control of all the Gaza Strip," Netanyahu vowed Monday in a video released by his office announcing that Israel would begin delivering "minimal humanitarian aid: food and medicine only." Netanyahu claimed that international pressure, including from pro-Israel Republican senators and the White House, required the appearance of humanitarian intervention. "Our best friends in the world — senators I know as strong supporters of Israel — have warned that they cannot support us if images of mass starvation emerge," he said. "They come to me and say, 'We'll give you all the help you need to win the war... but we can't be receiving pictures of famine,'" Netanyahu added. To continue the war of annihilation, he asserted, "We need to do it in a way that they won't stop us."

As usual, Israeli Finance Minister Bezalel Smotrich went even further in saying the quiet part out loud and giving the whole game away, explaining that Israel is providing just enough aid to maintain western support and avoid war crimes charges while advancing its ethnic cleansing operation in the Gaza Strip, boasting about the government's skillfulness in "navigating" that line.

Some choice Smotrich quotes, courtesy of the aforementioned Drop Site News write-up:

> Smotrich said the aid scheme would allow "our friends in the world to continue to provide us with an international umbrella of protection against the Security Council and the Hague Tribunal, and for us to continue to fight, God willing, until victory."

> "The [aid] that will enter Gaza in the coming days is the tiniest amount. A handful of bakeries that will hand out pita bread to

people in public kitchens. People in Gaza will get a pita and a food plate, and that's it. Exactly what we are seeing in the videos: people standing in line and waiting to have someone serve them, with some soup plate."

"Truth be told, until the last of the hostages returns, we should also not let water into the Gaza Strip. But the reality is that if we do that, the world will force us to halt the war immediately, and to lose. It would be winning the battle, and losing the war. I'm committed to winning the war."

"We are disassembling Gaza, and leaving it as piles of rubble, with total destruction [which has] no precedent globally. And the world isn't stopping us. There are pressures. There are those who attack [us]; they are trying to [make us] stop; they are not succeeding. You know why they aren't succeeding? Because we are navigating [the campaign] responsibly and wisely, and that's how we'll continue to do [it]."

Smotrich said that the Israeli forces are initiating a campaign to force Palestinians into the south of Gaza "and from there, God willing, to third countries, as part of President Trump's plan. This is a change of the course of history — nothing less."

Smotrich also praised the IDF for deliberately targeting civilians and civil infrastructure, saying "The IDF is finally conducting a campaign against the civilian rule of Hamas… eliminating ministers, officials, money changers, and figures in the economic and governmental apparatus."

So there you have it, spelled out in plain language. There is no need to wonder why Israel has been dragging out its genocidal atrocities over a year and a half instead of just brazenly annihilating all the Palestinians in one swift scorched-earth campaign. Israel has told us why. They have opted for their slow-motion strangulation approach because that's what's necessary to maintain essential western support and avoid war crimes tribunals.

This comes as the governments of France, Canada and the UK publicly issue a warning to Israel saying that they may begin imposing targeted sanctions on Tel Aviv if it does not begin allowing in more aid to Gaza and curbing the abuses in the West Bank. So Israel is currently acutely aware that it is walking a delicate line between (A) making Gaza an unlivable hellhole for Palestinians and (B) maintaining western support. So it is making the smallest concessions it thinks it can get away with in order to keep both A and B.

The western pushback against Israel's criminality has thus far been feeble, pathetic, and entirely inadequate. Australia's denunciation of Israel's starvation warfare is even more toothless than that of France, the UK and Canada. But we are seeing some movement, which shows that these western governments are not entirely unresponsive to internal pressures from their citizenry.

I just saw a tweet from the Quincy Institute's Trita Parsi which reads as follows:

"Something is happening. The number of government officials from around the world who I've heard in private conversations call Israel's slaughter in Gaza a genocide — without qualifications and caveats — has increased dramatically in just the past weeks. The dam is breaking."

Keep pushing.

•

The World Cannot Know True Peace Until We Have Reckoned With What We Did To Gaza

I was listening to a young writer describe an idea he'd had that he was so excited about he couldn't sleep the night before, and I remembered how before Gaza I used to get excited about writing stuff. I haven't felt that feeling since 2023.

I'm not complaining or feeling sorry for myself, I'm just remarking on how incredibly bleak and dark the world has been during this terrible time. It would be weird and unhealthy if I was enjoying my job here this past year and a half. These things aren't supposed to feel good. Not if you're really looking at them and being sincere and honest with yourself about what you are seeing.

It's been so ugly and so unsettling this whole time. There's not really any way to reframe all this horror and make it okay. All you can do is work on yourself to make sure you have enough inner spaciousness to accommodate the bad feelings and feel them all the way through until they've had their say. Let in the despair. The grief. The rage. The pain. Let it move all the way through your system without resisting and then get up and write the next thing.

That's what writing is for me now. It's never anything I am excited to share or am lit up with inspiration about. If anything it's more like "Okay, here you go, awful sorry I've got to show this to you, folks." It's just staring into the darkness and the blood and the gore and the anguished faces and writing out what I see, day after day.

Nothing about it is pleasant or rewarding. It's just what you do when there's a live-streamed genocide happening right in front of you with the backing of your own society. Everything about it sucks, and there's no way to make it not suck, but you do what needs to be done, like you would if it were your own family out there in the rubble.

This genocide has changed me forever. It has changed a lot of people forever. We will never be the same. The world will never be the same. No matter what happens or how this nightmare ends, things are never again going back to the way they were.

And they shouldn't. The Gaza holocaust is the product of the way the world was before it happened. Our society birthed it into existence, and now it's staring us all right in the face. This is who we are. This is the fruit of the tree of what western civilization has been up until this point.

Now it's just a matter of doing everything we can to make sure the genocide ends, and that the world learns the right lessons from it. This is as worthy a cause as anyone could take up in this life.

I still have hope that we can have a healthy world. I still have hope that writing about what's happening can be enjoyable again one day. But these things exist on the other side of some very hard and confronting work in the years to come. There's just no getting around it. The world cannot have peace and happiness until we have fully reckoned with what we did to Gaza.

•

Israel Is A Uniquely Evil Society
•Notes From The Edge Of The Narrative Matrix•

A former Knesset member named Moshe Feiglin went on Israeli television on Tuesday and proclaimed that "every child, every baby in Gaza is an enemy" of Israel, and that "not a single Gazan child will be left there" after Israel's genocidal onslaught is completed.

"Every child, every baby in Gaza is an enemy," Feiglin said. "The enemy is not Hamas, nor is it the military wing of Hamas, as our military commander tells us, that we are forbidden to harm a Hamasnik unless he is part of the military wing."

"Every child in Gaza is the enemy," Feiglin reiterated. "We need to occupy Gaza and settle it, and not a single Gazan child will be left there. There is no other victory."

This comes as the United Nations urgently warns that Israel still isn't allowing aid into Gaza, posing an immediate threat to the lives of thousands of babies.

Israel is a uniquely evil society. I don't think that's an unfair or unreasonable thing to say. Many other nations do evil things and many other nations have murderous extremists, but what other nations have their own mainstream politicians saying this sort of thing on mainstream television? I can't think of any.

A new poll shared by Israel's Channel 13 News found that most Israelis still don't believe their government has to allow humanitarian aid into Gaza. It's not just the leaders. It's not just the fringe wingnuts. It's a whole country full of sociopaths. Israel's atrocities in Gaza are the result of what Israelis are as a collective. The entire nation is heartless and fucked in the head.

•

Axios' Barak Ravid has published yet another anonymously sourced article claiming the US president is "frustrated" with Netanyahu, only this time the president is Trump.

Ravid is an Israeli intelligence insider who during the Biden administration spearheaded the freakish trend in US news media of churning out articles which insinuated that the president may be just moments away from breaking with the Israeli government and halting the Gaza genocide — a claim which according to Israel's then-ambassador to the United States was never anywhere close to being true.

Ravid reports that "President Trump has been frustrated by the ongoing war in Gaza and upset by images of suffering of Palestinian children, and has told his aides to tell Israeli Prime Minister Benjamin Netanyahu he wants him to wrap it up."

Which sounds awesome until you remember that Ravid has also printed such lines as:

> "A U.S. official said this part of last Saturday's call between the two leaders was one of the most difficult and 'frustrating' conversations Biden has had with Netanyahu since the beginning of the war in Gaza. It's a sign of the growing tensions between Biden and Netanyahu." (December 2023)

> "President Biden and other senior U.S. officials are becoming increasingly frustrated with Israeli Prime Minister Benjamin Netanyahu and his rejection of most of the administration's recent requests related to the war in Gaza." (January 2024)

> "Biden has grown increasingly frustrated with Netanyahu and Israel's actions during the war. The U.S. president earlier this month called the Israeli military operation in Gaza 'over the top' and in January he told Netanyahu he's not in it for a year of war." (February 2024)

> "The U.S. officials say Biden — and many other senior officials at the White House and the State Department — are extremely frustrated by what they see as ungratefulness by Netanyahu." (March 2024)

The list just goes on and on and on and on. It's month after month after month of this schtick. Who does this guy think he's kidding? This isn't journalism, it's propaganda. He's just providing the public with false assurance and buying time for Israel to complete its genocide.

•

And now we're getting reports that Israel is preparing to attack Iranian nuclear facilities if Tehran's negotiations with Washington don't go the way it likes. Something's got to be done about this maniacal regime.

•

The Washington Post has published an article titled "Biden was empath-in-chief. Can a divided country offer him empathy?", subtitled "In the face of Biden's cancer diagnosis, does the country have the capacity for empathy despite the political rancor, distrust, alternative facts and lies?"

These lines about a genocidal monster sum up everything I hate about the mainstream media, and liberals, and western civilization all at once.

•

I wish for Joe Biden what he has always wished for the Palestinians. I wish for everyone what they wish for the Palestinians. No more, no less. Just exactly what they wish for.

•

The Western Media Brought Gaza To This Point

Benjamin Netanyahu is now explicitly saying that the complete ethnic cleansing of Gaza is a precondition to ending the slaughter in the besieged Palestinian territory.

The Times of Israel reports:

> "Responding to those who are pushing for an end to war in Gaza, Netanyahu says he 'is ready to end the war, under clear conditions that will ensure the safety of Israel — all the hostages come home, Hamas lays down its arms, steps down from power, its leadership is exiled from the Strip… Gaza is totally disarmed, and we carry out the Trump plan. A plan that is so correct and so revolutionary.'
>
> "This represents the first time the US president's plan for moving Gaza civilians out of the Strip has been presented as an Israeli demand for ending the war."

Trump's stated plan for Gaza is to remove "all" Palestinians from the enclave and never allow them to return. Netanyahu is here saying that the ethnic cleansing of Gaza is Israel's ultimate military objective.

Which has been obvious from the very beginning. On the 20th of October 2023, a mere 13 days after October 7, I myself posted the following:

> "Israel's being so obvious about wanting to do another land grab.

The solution to every problem is to move Gazans off the land they're on to somewhere else. It's like a guy at a nightclub pushing you and pushing you to drink a drink he handed you; at a certain point you realize he's probably not really interested in making sure you have enough to drink."

It's been so transparently obvious this entire time that Israel's entire objective is to remove Palestinians from a Palestinian territory so their land can be used for Israel's own purposes — but you'd never have known it from looking at the western press.

For the last year and a half the western media have been brazenly lying to the public by framing this as a "war with Hamas" instead of the naked ethnic cleansing operation it clearly is. They've been manufacturing consent for this murderous land grab by babbling about hostages, terrorism and October 7 when Israel's mass atrocity in Gaza has never, ever been about any of those things. It has only ever been about taking Palestinian land away from Palestinians — an agenda Israel has been pursuing for decades.

If the western press had been doing actual journalism, Israel would never have been able to bring Gaza to this point. Because the western press have instead been administering propaganda this entire time, Gaza is now an uninhabitable pile of rubble full of desperate, starving people, allowing Israel and the Trump administration to argue that the humanitarian thing to do is to evacuate them all immediately.

The western media's refusal to acknowledge this — combined with a year and a half of wildly biased headlines, indisputably slanted coverage, and extensively documented top-down pressure in mass media institutions to cover Israel's onslaught in a positive light — stifled much of the public opposition to this genocidal land grab that we would likely have seen otherwise. This journalistic malpractice allowed Israel's western backers to support this mass atrocity with impunity, which in turn allowed Israel to act with impunity.

None of this would be possible if the west had an actual free press whose job is to create an informed populace. But we do not have an actual free press whose job is to create an informed populace — we have imperial propaganda services disguised as news.

Now that Israel has pulled back the curtain and acknowledged what we are looking at here, some in the western press have begun pivoting to wag their fingers at Netanyahu in order to preserve their image. And fine, whatever, we need as much help as we can get. But never forget what these monsters did to help create this nightmare in Gaza.

•

Thoughts On The Israeli Embassy Staff Killings
•Notes From The Edge Of The Narrative Matrix•

Two staff members of the Israeli embassy in Washington DC have been shot and killed by a man who shouted "Free Palestine" and reportedly told police "I did it for Palestine, I did it for Gaza" after his arrest.

The entire western political/media class is ferociously decrying this as an antisemitic attack, despite the shooter's clear and unambiguous motives against the state of Israel rather than the Jewish faith, and despite one of the two victims being a Christian from Germany.

So let's get one thing clear from the beginning: two Israeli embassy staffers getting shot in Washington DC is less newsworthy than tens of thousands of Palestinians being killed in Israel's genocidal land grab. It is less important. It deserves less attention. It is not the main story. Israel's genocide in Gaza is the main story.

•

Many are suggesting that this was some kind of false flag attack to change the narrative and rescue Israel's image on the world stage as public sentiments turn against its genocidal atrocities. I see no evidence for this at this time. I've been predicting that Israel's atrocities in Gaza will give rise to violent extremist attacks, because that's just what happens when you do profoundly evil things in full view of the entire world. There may be nothing more to it than that.

•

You simply cannot give Israel sympathy. For anything. Ever. No matter what happens. Israel weaponizes sympathy; it uses any sympathy it's given as a weapon to justify murdering people. If someone uses something as a weapon to murder people, it's immoral to keep handing them weapons. You must disarm them.

•

The real story here is how the entire western political/media class has expressed more outrage and sympathy over the killing of two Israeli embassy staffers than tens of thousands of Palestinians in history's first live-streamed genocide. The coverage of the story **is** the story, because it exposes how little regard the western empire has for the lives of non-westerners. Palestinians are not regarded as fully human, so their deaths by daily genocidal massacres are considered less worthy of attention than a double homicide in Washington DC.

Western institutions regard Muslims and Arabs and people with darker skin as subhuman vermin whose extermination should be met with an emotional response ranging somewhere between indifference to glee. Our civilization views itself as morally superior to Nazi Germany while continuing basically the same atrocities under basically the same ideology.

That's the real story here. That's the real lesson.

•

So let's recap in case anyone's confused:

Nothing Israel did to Gaza justified October 7, but also October 7 justifies everything Israel has been doing in Gaza, but also nothing Israel has been doing in Gaza since October 7 justifies any violence toward Israel.

Everyone got that? Does that sound about right?

•

CNN's Dana Bash is already suggesting that "Free Palestine" is a call for violence against Jews, and ADL chief Jonathan Greenblatt is citing the embassy staff shooting as evidence of the need to deplatform pro-Palestine voices.

This comes as British police level terrorism charges against a member of the Irish hip hop trio Kneecap for waving a Hezbollah flag at a concert.

I have said it before and I will say it again: Zionism is the single greatest threat to free speech in our society today. The west's support for Israel is causing a nonstop aggressive assault on our civil rights throughout the entire western world. This is personal. Israel directly threatens us all.

•

Today's Hitler Says "Free Palestine" Is Today's "Heil Hitler"

Benjamin Netanyahu has wasted no time proclaiming that "Free Palestine is just today's version of Heil Hitler" following the shooting of two Israeli embassy staffers in Washington DC on Thursday, seizing on this new opportunity to frame Israel's critics as dangerous Jew haters who must be shut down by any means necessary.

Yeah sure, Bibi. Right. Opposing today's Hitler is today's version of Heil Hitler.

There's been a frenetic push from the pro-Israel crowd in using the slain embassy staffers to argue that pro-Palestine protesters need to be shut down, and it's just so ridiculous. Nobody should grant it even one second of serious consideration.

There is nothing that could possibly happen that would convince me it's wrong to oppose an active genocide.

No number of politically motivated assassinations will ever make me believe that opposing the Gaza holocaust is the wrong thing to do.

There is no amount of shrieking about "antisemitism" that would cause me to consider the possibility that maybe intentionally starving civilians is alright after all.

There is no amount of Israel apologists who could show up in my comments section calling me a Nazi that would ever make me believe it's okay to rain military explosives on a giant concentration camp full of children.

There is no amount of concern trolling the mass media could do to suggest that saying "Free Palestine" is violently radicalizing people that would ever make me change my mind about the immorality of intentionally annihilating hospitals and medical workers.

This is not a debate. My position is indisputably, unassailably, unshakably correct. It is correct from a moral standpoint. It is correct from a logical standpoint. It is correct from a factual standpoint. And it always will be.

Any time Israel's supporters find an excuse to milk a little more sympathy they all spend days going "Aha, see! Our genocide is good after all, and you are wrong to oppose it!" And the answer is always an immediate and unequivocal "Nope."

After the embassy staff shooting my various comments sections were flooded with Israel supporters frantically calling me every name in the book for saying those two deaths were less significant and newsworthy than the ongoing genocide. But they weren't really angry about what I said, they were angry that I was shitting on

their "See this means our genocide is fine" PR parade. That I was telling everyone not to play along with what the pro-Israel spin machine was about to try and do.

But I am right, and they are wrong. There is no valid argument to the contrary. A much more egregious act of violence could target Israel tomorrow, and I would still be completely and indisputably correct in opposing the genocidal atrocities in Gaza. Such acts could target Israel every single day thereafter, and I would still be completely and indisputably correct in opposing the genocidal atrocities in Gaza.

And there is nothing they could possibly say to me to convince me otherwise.

Nothing will ever cause me to believe that it is moral and reasonable to systematically murder Palestinians and make their territory uninhabitable in order to drive them off it and seize it. That will always be wrong, and everyone who says so will always be correct, no matter what happens. End of discussion. Forever.

•

It's A Complete Lie To Say Gaza Can Have Peace If Hamas Surrenders
•Notes From The Edge Of The Narrative Matrix•

Anyone who says Gaza will be at peace if Hamas just surrenders and releases the hostages is either knowingly sowing disinformation or ignorantly sowing misinformation. We need to make sure everyone's clear on this so nobody can say they didn't know after history unpacks this one.

Netanyahu has made it completely and unambiguously clear that even if Hamas surrendered today and released every single hostage, Trump's ethnic cleansing plan will still need to be implemented as a precondition for ending the mass slaughter. To be absolutely 100 percent clear, Trump's plan for Gaza is that "all" Palestinians be removed on a "permanent" basis, never allowed to return.

There is no way to permanently remove all Palestinians from a Palestinian territory without material coercion — meaning more mass scale violence and siege warfare. There is also no way to argue that this mass displacement would be voluntary even without further violence, since Israel has been deliberately and systematically making the Gaza Strip uninhabitable by destroying civilian infrastructure. Forcing them to choose between starvation in an uninhabitable wasteland or submit to ethnic cleansing is exactly the same as forcing them out at gunpoint.

It was obvious that this was Israel's plan for Gaza in October 2023; plans to move the civilian population out of the enclave were already being circulated within days of the onslaught. But that wasn't Israel's official and openly stated policy until the Trump administration; now that Israel is clearly and explicitly stating this agenda in public, there is absolutely no excuse for anyone to continue circulating the lie that the suffering of the people of Gaza ends if Hamas surrenders. What happens is that their homeland will be permanently taken away from them as they are shipped off to a foreign land, and Gaza will cease to exist as a Palestinian territory.

That's not peace. Or if it is it's the peace of an empty room; the peace of a room full of corpses. Saying you made peace by removing the Palestinians from Palestine is like saying you settled an argument by decapitating one of the arguers.

That's the only "peace" the people of Palestine will experience if Hamas lays down its arms. Losing everything they've ever known forever, on pain of death.

That is the inconvenient truth people are trying to hide when they say "This all ends when Hamas surrenders and releases the hostages." That is the deception they are sowing.

•

37

Israel bombed the home of two married doctors in Gaza on Friday, killing nine of their children and critically injuring their sole surviving son. The father of the children was also severely injured in the attack, while their mother, while still working at the nearby hospital, received the charred bodies of her children. They were too badly burned to be recognized.

This one incident, just by itself, is vastly more newsworthy and deserving of attention than two Israeli embassy staff members being killed in Washington. But news coverage hasn't reflected this, because Palestinians aren't regarded as human beings in the mainstream western press.

•

The Guardian has published an opinion piece by Rhiannon Lucy Cosslett titled "As Gaza's children are bombed and starved, we watch — powerless. What is it doing to us as a society?", which is noteworthy because it somehow never mentions the word "Israel" or "Israeli" one single time throughout the entire article. It doesn't even mention Netanyahu.

This is a particularly glaring example of the way the western press have been discussing the Gaza holocaust as some kind of unfortunate tragedy that is just passively happening to the Palestinian people, as though it's a natural disaster or something. It's

like bombs and siege warfare are just the weather over there. Like "Oh it's a bit bomby and faminy in Gaza today, and it makes me feel sad!"

This genocide is exposing the mass media like nothing else in my lifetime.

•

Israel supporters have different packages of apologia for each ideological group, with different narratives explaining why Israel's abuses are justified to all the different groups in language designed to appeal to each faction.

Are you a progressive humanitarian? Israel apologists have a narrative package custom designed to appeal to your support for the Jewish people and the revulsion you feel toward their historic persecution.

Are you a conservative who's fearful of Muslims and terrorism? Israel apologists have a completely different package of narratives designed to appeal to your fears and explain why Islamic extremism must be defeated to protect western civilization.

Are you a fundamentalist Christian? There's a whole other package of narratives designed to explain why support for Israel is actually commanded by God in the Holy Bible.

Are you a fascist who thinks Arabs should be wiped off the face of the earth? Boy howdy do the Israel apologists ever have some narratives for you.

Israel apologists understand that different political factions are responsive to different types of messaging, so each political faction gets its own messaging package.

The only ones they can't effectively target with carefully constructed narratives are the groups who are already forcefully pro-Palestine, predominantly on the leftmost end of the political spectrum. So they just work on silencing, stigmatizing and marginalizing those groups instead.

It's all about controlling the narrative. Israel apologists understand the power of narrative control better than perhaps any other major ideological faction on earth, and you see it at play throughout every facet of our society. That's one of the many reasons they were so successful at manufacturing support for Israel in the west up until history's first live-streamed genocide caused them to finally start losing control of the story.

•

If You Don't Oppose The Gaza Holocaust, You've Been Wasting Your Life On This Planet

They're burning kids alive in Gaza. They're burning them alive. And still people are silent, or are actively supporting Israel, or are spouting mealy-mouthed both-sides gibberish while shrugging their shoulders.

A spiritual teacher who I used to like posted the most obnoxious screed today babbling about how both Israelis and Palestinians are suffering in this "war" and that, while Israel does have a "right to defend itself", it's time for a ceasefire to be reached.

This is a guy who's made a career out of presenting himself as so wise, insightful and enlightened that people should pay him money to hear what he has to say about life and spiritual attainment, finally deciding to speak out about a genocide that's been going on for nearly 20 months now, and saying the most vapid, infantile nonsense imaginable. I know teenagers who could've done a much better job.

And from where I'm sitting, if this is the best you can do after a lifetime dedicated to spiritual insight and awakening, then what good was any of it? If you can't even take a solid stance against history's first live-streamed genocide after decades of spiritual seeking and spiritual finding, then it kinda seems like you've been wasting your life this whole time.

And I guess I feel pretty much the same way about everyone who still isn't taking a stand on this thing. This is not a complicated issue. It doesn't take a tremendous amount of learning, wisdom or morality to wind up on the correct side of this thing. You don't have to be a buddha, a scholar or a saint to oppose an active genocide. You just have to not be all fucked up inside.

There is only one correct position to have on the Gaza holocaust, and if you still haven't managed to find your way into that position then I think it's fair to say you have been wasting your life on this planet up until this point.

I mean, what have you even been doing here exactly? You clearly haven't been working on becoming a decent person. You haven't been learning about the world. You haven't been expanding your awareness of justice and inequality. You haven't been working on developing a truth-based relationship with reality. You haven't been developing empathy for your fellow human beings. You haven't been growing or maturing. What exactly have you been doing? How have you managed to spend your entire life avoiding all the most important things about living as a human organism on this planet?

It's not too late to change this, of course. It's never too late to change. If you still haven't taken your stand against the genocide in Gaza, you can change this right away. If you don't know enough about what's happening, get curious and start learning. If you're having trouble discerning fact from fiction, get humble and ask questions. If you're having trouble sorting out right from wrong, get quiet inside and look in your heart. You've got this.

You don't need any special qualifications to speak out against the Gaza holocaust. You are already fully qualified to do so. Many people far more ignorant and far less ethical than yourself are already speaking out in support of Israel's actions, so you should feel free to use your own voice just as loudly. Learn as much as you can, but don't feel like you need to be some kind of expert to speak out against a genocide that's been facilitated by your own government.

Get moving on this. There's no time to lose. Children are burning, and the clock is running out. Take a firm position on the great moral issue of our time, or be prepared to spend the rest of your life explaining why you didn't.

•

This Dystopia Would Never Be Accepted Without Extensive Indoctrination

I am not a politically complicated person. I think genocide is bad. I think peace is good. I don't think anyone should be struggling to survive in a civilization that is capable of providing for all. I think we should try to preserve the biosphere we all depend on for survival.

To me these are just obvious, common sense positions, no more remarkable or profound than believing I should refrain from slamming my nipple in a car door. I do not think these views should put me on the political fringe. I don't think they should cause me to be seen as some kind of radical. It's not outlandish that I hold these views, it's outlandish that everyone else does not.

But that's the kind of society we find ourselves in today. The obvious is framed as freakish while the freakish is presented as obvious. Health is framed as sickness while sickness is presented as health. The moderate is framed as extremism while extremism is presented as moderate.

We live in a twisted, backwards dystopia where everything is the opposite of the way it should be, and we're conditioned to think it's normal and acceptable. It's not until some degree of insight dawns in you that you look around and realize you are living in the nightmare of a madman. Until then you spend your time here thinking, speaking, voting and behaving as though the demented status quo we are living under is the moderate and expected reality.

All our lives we are trained to believe this hellscape is the healthy and expected circumstance for our species. Our parents and teachers tell us that it's normal for things to be this way. Our pundits and politicians assure us that there's no other way things could be and that we are living under the best possible system.

A big part of it is just growing up in a society that's been diseased since long before you were born, being raised and taught by people who also grew up in a society that's been diseased since long before they were born. We show up here, we don't know anything, and then the big people teach us about war and money and jobs and politics, and assure us that our initial horrified reaction to the things we are learning is just immature naivety to something fine and normal.

If you've ever had the misfortune of having to explain war to a child, then you know how insane this civilization looks when perceived by a pair of fresh eyes. I've never had to explain the genocide in Gaza to a young child, but I am sure it would be met with even more shock and grief. Kids have a natural, healthy revulsion toward such things, and it is only by sustained indoctrination that we are able to twist their minds into seeing them as normal.

It takes a lot of education to make us this stupid. Our minds require a whole lot of training to accept this horrific dystopia as the baseline norm. That's why the empire we live under has the most sophisticated domestic propaganda machine that has ever existed.

In order to have clarity, we need to learn to look with fresh eyes. Uninitiated eyes. Eyes that have not been educated out of their initial healthy impulse to weep at what we are doing and how we are living here. We need to get in touch with that intuition within us which rejects the sickness of our society as though it was meeting it for the very first time.

Learning to meet life afresh in each instant is good practice anyway; it makes living a lot more enjoyable and beautiful, and it helps us move in a much wiser way since we're not constantly reacting to old patterns and expectations in an ever-changing world. But as an added bonus it also peels away the tolerance we have built up for the backwards lunacy of this empire we are living under.

The less healthy this civilization feels to you, the healthier you are getting. Everything about this nightmare looks appalling through clear eyes.

•

Sorry If This Is Antisemitic But I Think It's Wrong To Burn Children Alive
•Notes From The Edge Of The Narrative Matrix•

Israel is burning children alive in Gaza. And call me an antisemitic Jew-hating Nazi terrorist lover if you must, but I happen to believe that's wrong.

•

Now that it's been made clear that Israel's goal in Gaza is the complete ethnic cleansing of all Palestinians, Israel apologists have been shifting from bleating about hostages and Hamas to arguing that ethnic cleansing is actually fine and good. Which makes sense; that's really the only argument they can make at this point.

•

Never forget that the US Congress gave Netanyahu dozens of standing ovations during a single speech while he was in the middle of perpetrating history's first live-streamed genocide. This is who they are. It will always be who they are.

•

Israel has done more to promote hatred toward Jews in the last year and a half than Stormfront has in its entire existence. No white supremacist propaganda will ever be as effective at spreading hatred against Jews as openly mass murdering children under a Star of David flag.

•

Support for Israel used to be the overwhelmingly dominant opinion in the western world. Luckily that's changing, but the fact that this was the case until Israel exposed itself shows you really can't just go along with majority opinion on any issue. You need to think for yourself.

Ignore what the crowd says. Ignore people who scream at you for disagreeing with their position. Look at the raw facts as free from your own cognitive biases as you are able, and have the courage to stand on your own if necessary.

•

Gaza is such an easy moral issue to get right that there's no way anyone who gets it wrong isn't a shitty person in other areas of their life as well. I feel sorry for anyone who has interpersonal relationships with Israel supporters, because they'd suck to be around.

•

World Food Programme director Cindy McCain is saying that she's seen no evidence of Hamas stealing aid entering Gaza. Israel's one and only argument for continuing to block aid to Gaza is being publicly debunked by a member of one of the most pro-Israel families in US politics.

•

The US has reportedly delivered some 90,000 tons of weapons to Israel since October 2023.

I mostly focus on the Gaza genocide these days, but sometimes figures like this make me zoom out a few clicks and think about how bat shit insane our civilization is as a whole. Just think how much good we could do in the world if we weren't pouring resources into evil shit like this.

•

Murdoch-owned publication The Australian came after me the other day for tweeting "Two Israeli embassy staff getting shot in Washington DC is less newsworthy than tens of thousands of Palestinians being killed in Israel's genocidal land grab. It is less important. It deserves less attention. It is not the main story. Israel's genocide in Gaza is the main story."

They called me a "journalist" in scare quotes, which I guess is supposed to be an insult, but coming from the Murdoch press it can only be seen as a compliment.

•

According to the official western narrative, Americans becoming violently radicalized by a US-backed genocide is a bigger issue than the US-backed genocide.

According to the official narrative, university protests against a transparent ethnic cleansing operation are a greater concern than the transparent ethnic cleansing operation.

According to the official narrative, western Zionist Jews feeling emotionally upset about opposition to a modern-day holocaust is a more urgent problem than a modern-day holocaust.

All of our institutions are backwards and evil. Our media. Our politics. Our education system. Our manufacturers of mainstream culture. This should be clear to everyone by now.

Every historical evil we were taught never to repeat is being repeated by our own rulers.

Everything we were taught to fear about the countries that the western empire hates is true of the western empire.

Every dark future we were warned about in dystopian fiction is true of the dystopia we are living in presently.

We live in a nightmare of a civilization, under an empire that is fueled by human blood. The closer you examine it, the uglier it gets.

This cannot be allowed to continue. It must not be allowed to continue.

The empire must fall.

If This Is What Israel Does, Then Israel Shouldn't Exist

Gaza's youngest social media influencer has been killed by Israeli forces after touching tens of thousands of lives with her stories of survival in the besieged Palestinian territory. Her name was Yaqeen Hammad. She was 11 years old.

Israeli forces fired upon starving civilians in Gaza on Tuesday when they rushed inside a facility holding aid, reportedly killing three and wounding dozens more. The facility was operated by the Gaza Humanitarian Foundation, the latest US-Israeli scheme to bypass normal UN aid distribution and lure Gaza's population into specific concentrated locations.

A new report from the Associated Press confirms that Israeli forces have been using Palestinians as human shields in Gaza as a matter of policy. This is actually using human shields in the very real sense of deliberately forcing civilians between yourself and potential enemy fire, not in the fake sense of being somewhere near civilians as per the made-up "human shields" narrative that Israel uses to blame its daily massacres on Hamas.

A survey of Jewish Israelis conducted by an Israeli polling firm has found that 82 percent of respondents support the total ethnic cleansing of Gaza, and 47 percent believe Israeli forces should kill every man, woman and child in every city they capture there.

Haaretz reports on the poll's findings:

"Sixty-five percent said they believed in the existence of a modern-day incarnation of Amalek, the Israelite biblical enemy whom God commanded to wipe out in Deuteronomy 25:19. Among those believers, 93 percent said the commandment to erase Amalek's memory remains relevant today."

These are just a few reports from the past few days, on top of all the other staggeringly evil things that Israel has been doing this whole time.

If this is Israel, then Israel should not exist. If what we are seeing in Gaza is what it means for Israel to exist, then it shouldn't.

People scream bloody murder when you say this, but it shouldn't be a controversial position. I'm not saying Jews shouldn't exist, I'm saying a genocidal apartheid state should not exist. A state is an artificial construct of the human mind, held together by human actions. If the actions we are witnessing in Gaza are the product of the artificial construct of the Israeli state, then that artificial construct should be dismantled, and those actions should cease.

I would say this about any other man-made construct that is doing the things Israel is doing. If some scientists built a robot that spends all day every day massacring children, then I would say the robot should be unmade. If you drew a Star of David on the robot's head, it wouldn't suddenly make me an evil antisemite to say that the child-murdering robot should be dismantled.

Dismantling the apartheid state of Israel would mean granting everyone citizenship and equal rights, allowing right of return, denazifying apartheid culture, paying extensive reparations, and righting the wrongs of the past. You could still call what remains "Israel" if you wanted to, but it would be nothing like the state that presently exists under that name.

Would this upset the feelings of some Jewish people? Yes. Would it inconvenience the lives of some Jewish people? Certainly. But that would be infinitely preferable to the daily massacres, genocidal atrocities and reckless regional warmongering we are witnessing from the state of Israel. Advocating the end of this genocidal state doesn't make someone a monster, advocating its continuation does. The only way to believe otherwise is to take it as a given that Palestinian lives are worth less than Jewish feelings.

Israel is currently presenting nonstop arguments for its own cessation. Every video that comes out showing Israelis acting in monstrous ways and innocent Palestinians being murdered, tortured and abused in the most horrific ways imaginable is an argument for which there is no verbal counter-argument. Every day that goes by, the genocidal apartheid state of Israel is proving to the world that it should not exist.

Gaza's Hospitals ARE The Target

It's a relatively well-known fact that Israeli forces have attacked the overwhelming majority of hospitals in Gaza and have launched hundreds upon hundreds of strikes on medical services in the enclave.

Whenever anyone mentions this fact publicly they'll get Israel apologists babbling about "human shields" and absurdly trying to claim that there are Hamas bases in all the hospitals. But these talking points are invalidated by the fact that we've seen multiple reports from doctors documenting Israeli forces actually entering hospitals they've attacked and destroying all the individual pieces of medical equipment in those facilities, one by one.

The latest of such reports appears in the Greek outlet Efimerida ton Syntakton from a specialist surgeon named Christos Georgalas, who was at Nasser Hospital in Khan Yunis in southern Gaza from April to May of this year.

According to machine translation, Georgalas calls Israel's onslaught "a war mainly against children," and describes horrific injuries that Israeli munitions have been inflicting upon young Palestinians.

Georgalas also describes repeated Israeli attacks on the hospital where he was working, which include the following:

"A Spanish colleague told me that when the Israelis came to the hospital where the MRI machine was, they tried to destroy everything. But the MRI machine is a huge machine. It's like a car. Even if you shoot it, it can be repaired. So they brought in a specialist engineer to permanently destroy it. Because even if a bomb went off next to it, it could still be repaired. They had to bring in a specialist who knew the heart of the machine to make it non-functional. And that's exactly what he did last February.

"In our hospital, the Israelis went through the wards that were the incubators and systematically broke them one by one. The incubators with the crowbar! This has been recorded by my colleagues. The hospital where I worked was occupied by the Israelis for two months, in February and March 2024. The doctors who had remained in the hospital were tortured. They were lined up one by one and beaten. A total of around 80 of them were kidnapped. Of these, we do not know where 40 are or if they are alive. They killed many on the spot."

Because Israel has been blocking journalists from entering the Gaza Strip, doctors have largely become the de facto reporters on the ground there.

We saw another report documenting Israel's pattern of systematically destroying individual pieces of medical equipment back in February of this year, this time at the Indonesian Hospital in northern Gaza. Doctors Without Borders emergency coordinator Caroline Seguin reported the following:

"There is no health system anymore in the northern part of Gaza. Kamal Adwan hospital has been razed, while Al Shifa, Al Awda and Indonesian hospitals are seriously damaged and only partially functioning. We were utterly shocked to observe that in Indonesian hospital every medical machine seemed to have been deliberately destroyed; they were smashed to pieces, one by one, to make sure no medical care could be provided anymore. You have to ask: What is the motivation of such action? These machines are made to save people's lives, mothers, fathers, children. It's devastating to see the state of these hospitals."

In April of this year Seguin's report on the Indonesian Hospital was corroborated by an emergency physician named Clayton Dalton, who wrote the following for The New Yorker:

"Sultan led me upstairs, to the I.C.U., where wind blew through broken windows. He wanted to show me something that he had discovered after Israeli forces left the hospital. He pointed to a cardiac monitor near a wall. It appeared to have a bullet hole in its screen. Next to it was an EKG machine whose screen had been smashed.

"We entered a large storage room in the corner of the I.C.U. which was crammed with medical devices: ultrasound machines, I.V. pumps, dialysis machines, blood-pressure monitors. Each had apparently been destroyed by a bullet — not in a pattern one would expect from random shooting but, rather, methodically. I was stunned. I couldn't think of any possible military justification for destroying lifesaving equipment."

Indeed, there is no possible military justification for destroying lifesaving medical equipment. They were destroyed so that they could not be used to save lives. Israel has been systematically destroying Gaza's healthcare infrastructure with the goal of making it uninhabitable, so that the territory can be seized by Israel.

That's three separate accounts describing Israeli forces systematically destroying medical equipment in Gaza, from doctors who'd stand nothing to gain from lying about such a thing. The evidence is too overwhelming to deny.

There were no Hamas fighters hiding in the MRI machine. There were no tunnels in the incubators. No arms stockpiles in the EKG machine. Israel has been lying about Hamas hiding in hospitals this entire time. Hamas was never the target. Hospitals are the target. Healthcare is the target. That's established far beyond any reasonable doubt by now.

•

https://www.caitlinjohnst.one

www.ingramcontent.com/pod-product-compliance
Lightning Source LLC
Chambersburg PA
CBHW081204270326
41930CB00014B/3301